experience and a passion for tr...

Rely on Thomas Cook as your travelling companion on your next trip and benefit from our unique heritage.

Thomas Cook **pocket** guides

NEWCASTLE

Written by Paul Shawcross

Published by Thomas Cook Publishing
A division of Thomas Cook Tour Operations Limited
Company registration no. 3772199 England
The Thomas Cook Business Park, Unit 9, Coningsby Road,
Peterborough PE3 8SB, United Kingdom
Email: books@thomascook.com, Tel: +44 (0) 1733 416477
www.thomascookpublishing.com

Produced by Cambridge Publishing Management Limited
Burr Elm Court, Main Street, Caldecote CB23 7NU
www.cambridgepm.co.uk

ISBN: 978-1-84848-462-7

This first edition © 2010 Thomas Cook Publishing
Text © Thomas Cook Publishing
Cartography supplied by Redmoor Design, Tavistock, Devon
Map data © OpenStreetMap contributors CC–BY–SA; www.openstreetmap.org,
www.creativecomments.org
Transport map © Nexus

Series Editor: Karen Beaulah
Production/DTP: Steven Collins

Printed and bound in Spain by GraphyCems

Cover photography © Thomas Cook Publishing

CONTENTS

SYMBOLS KEY

The following symbols are used throughout this book:

a address **t** telephone **f** fax **w** website address **e** email
c opening times **N** public transport connections **!** important

The following symbols are used on the maps:

i	information office	■	points of interest
✈	airport	O	city
✚	hospital	O	large town
⊙	police station	○	small town
▤	bus station	=	motorway
▤	railway station	—	main road
M	metro	—	minor road
✝	cathedral	—	railway
1	numbers denote featured cafés, restaurants & venues

PRICE CATEGORIES

The ratings below indicate average price rates for a double room per night, including breakfast:
£ under £100 ££ £100–150 £££ over £150
The typical cost for a three-course meal without drinks, is as follows:
£ under £20 ££ £20–40 £££ over £40

▶ *Grey's Monument inscription*

THIS COLUMN WAS ERECTED IN
TO COMMEMORATE
THE SERVICES RENDERED TO HIS COUNTRY BY
HARLES, EARL GREY, K.
WHO, DURING AN ACTIVE POLITICAL CAREER OF
NEARLY HALF A CENTURY
WAS THE CONSTANT ADVOCATE OF PEACE
ND THE FEARLESS AND CONSISTENT CHAMPIO
CIVIL AND RELIGIOUS LIBERTY
E FIRST DIRECTED HIS EFFORTS TO THE AMEND
OF THE REPRESENTATION OF THE PEOPLE IN
AND WAS THE MINISTER
AND UNDER WHOSE GUID
AMENTARY RE

INTRODUCING
Newcastle

Introduction

The iconic bridges across the River Tyne, watched over by a magnificent medieval castle and flanked by the architectural masterpiece of The Sage Gateshead, set the scene for what is one of the finest and most amazing cities in the United Kingdom. Both first-time and regular visitors alike, especially if they arrive by train from the south, cannot fail to be impressed by the sight of these magnificent structures, which say so much about the city and its inhabitants.

Newcastle was founded in Roman times simply as a bridge across the river. This Roman structure has long since disappeared, although the piers were probably used for its medieval replacement. An obvious crossing-point over the River Tyne, its more recent bridges have featured prominently in its history, from the dual-purpose road and rail High Level, built by the celebrated railway engineer Robert Stephenson, right up to the striking, recently constructed Millennium Bridge or Blinking Eye.

Now a bustling university city, with first-class shopping, a vibrant nightlife, and a dynamic population of about 275,000 Geordies, Newcastle covers a relatively small area that can easily be explored on foot. The heart of the city is Grainger Town, which includes some magnificent neoclassical streets, in particular Grey Street; this is dominated by the impressive Grey's Monument, which commemorates one of the northeast's most famous sons, the former Prime Minister Earl Grey. Stretching away down towards the river, Grey Street came third in the 2010 Google Street View in the 'British Picturesque' category.

Some of the must-see places in the area are actually across the river in Gateshead. It is a curious anomaly that Newcastle and Gateshead, which stand opposite each other on the north and south banks respectively of the Tyne, have remained separate entities – except for a brief period in Tudor times, unlike most other similar pairs of settlements throughout the world, which have amalgamated at some point in their histories. Interestingly though, in recent years, Newcastle City Council and Gateshead Council have created the concept of 'NewcastleGateshead', which greatly simplifies the matter as far as visitors are concerned.

⬥ *The bridges at dusk*

When to go

SEASONS & CLIMATE

The climate of the northeast of England is a little cooler than areas to the south, especially during the summer. Average winter temperatures are around 3–5°C (37–41°F), while the summer average is around 15°C (59°F), although it may reach the high 20s (up to 80°F).

ANNUAL EVENTS

Newcastle has major events throughout the year. All the museums and galleries have special events and temporary exhibitions at various times, which they announce on their websites.

In late January to mid-February, starting at the ceremonial arch, Stowell Street and the surrounding areas of Chinatown are transformed with dragon, lion and unicorn dances to celebrate **Chinese New Year**.

On the last weekend of March, jazz aficionados flock to The Sage for the **Gateshead International Jazz Festival**.

During the second weekend in May more than 35 cultural venues across Newcastle and Gateshead, normally closed in the evening, open their doors to the public for **The Late Shows**. The last weekend sees the Quayside set the stage for **Evolution**, the largest music festival in the northeast, with great bands and a fantastic atmosphere.

The **Eat! festival** in mid- to late June is dedicated to food and drink in the region, at locations all over Newcastle and Gateshead. At the end of the month **The Hoppings**, Europe's largest funfair, pitches up on Newcastle's Town Moor.

Gateshead Stadium hosts the **Aviva British Grand Prix Athletics** in mid-July, where some of the world's best athletes strut their stuff. The non-sporting can head for the Summertyne Festival, with events and performances on the Quayside at the end of the month to celebrate the coming of summer.

The third Sunday of September is the date for **The Great North Run**. The world's biggest half-marathon (from Newcastle to South Shields) attracts 50,000 runners each year, raising millions of pounds for charities.

The October half-term's **Juice Festival**, across various locations, is NewcastleGateshead's celebration of the creativity of children aged 0–18.

In December, the cities are transformed into a winter wonderland, with many events to astound and fascinate, including pantomimes, light switch-ons, an ice rink and markets.

⬤ *Springtime in Old Eldon Square*

History

The first recorded activity on the site is the building of a Roman bridge in AD 120. This gave rise to the name for the settlement that grew up on the north shore, Pons Aelius, or Bridge of Aelius, the family name of the Emperor Hadrian who commissioned the nearby 119 km- (74 mile-) long wall. Following the withdrawal of the Romans during the 5th century, local people continued to occupy the settlement, which became known as Monkchester.

Robert Curthose, son of William I, built a motte-and-bailey castle on the site in 1080, giving the settlement its name of

⬥ The Castle Keep (see page 58) stands high above the Quayside

'New Castle'. During medieval times Newcastle was in fact little more than a a defensive outpost against the Scots, and although there was some trade – notably in coal and wool – this was limited until the city walls were constructed early in the 14th century.

It was not until the Tudor era (1485 onwards) that border skirmishes became less frequent and, as a result, the local economy flourished. The coal industry rapidly expanded and Newcastle became the most important exporter of coal in the land, hence the expression 'carrying coals to Newcastle': spending a lot of effort on a pointless exercise. Later, Newcastle became a Royalist stronghold, at first supporting James I then, during the Jacobite rebellion, declaring for King George I. Some believe this is how the locals earned the sobriquet of 'Geordies', a diminutive form of the name George.

The Victorian era saw the real flowering of Newcastle. It played a major part in the Industrial Revolution and the commercial centre moved from the Quayside to Grainger Town, with the construction of magnificent new neoclassical streets. In 1882 Newcastle became a city, although locals continue to refer to 'the Toon', a dialect word for 'town'.

In modern times Newcastle has continued to develop and is now a cosmopolitan city with an interesting and well-preserved architectural heritage. While limited damage was inflicted by Hitler's bombers, in the 1960s a large part of the centre was demolished to make way for a new retail complex, Eldon Square. Despite coming in for much criticism at the time, in fact it helped to revitalise Newcastle and paved the way for the current exciting, modern city.

Culture

Newcastle has been an important cultural centre for more than 200 years, boasting fascinating museums, a fine theatre, a state-of-the-art music centre and a world-famous art gallery, not to mention the many smaller venues. At the heart of this cultural activity is the **Literary and Philosophical Society** (see pages 46–7), or the Lit & Phil as it is affectionately and officially known. Founded in the late 18th century, it is now the largest independent library outside London.

The imaginative **The Sage Gateshead** (see pages 60–61) and **BALTIC Centre for Contemporary Art** (see pages 59–60) on the south bank of the river demonstrate the determination of NewcastleGateshead to be at the forefront of the arts. More traditional tastes are catered for at the **Laing Art Gallery** (see page 46), the **Great North Museum: Hancock** (see page 70) and the **Discovery Museum** (see page 70), all of which offer something to interest all ages. For many, however, the jewel in the crown has to be the **Theatre Royal** (see pages 47–8), with its magnificent neoclassical façade, standing majestically in the heart of Grainger Town.

● *Statue of the Tyne God at the Civic Centre*

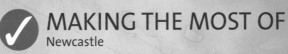 # MAKING THE MOST OF
Newcastle

Shopping

Eldon Square is one of the largest city-centre shopping complexes in the country. This is not the only place to shop, however, as the rest of the city centre is thronged with retailers of all descriptions. In the unlikely event that you run out of places to shop, there is also the nearby MetroCentre, Europe's largest indoor shopping mall, only a short bus or train ride away.

WHERE TO SHOP

Eldon Square is undoubtedly the main place to head on your shopping expedition and in all likelihood you'll find what you are looking for within its confines. It has recently been extended and remodelled and now, with the opening of the new St Andrew's Mall, covers 130,000 sq m (1.4 million sq ft). A four-storey Debenhams, two major department stores (John Lewis and Fenwick), a Marks & Spencer and a multitude of designer outlets provide a good choice. Adjoining Eldon Square are **Eldon Garden** and **Monument Mall** which offer a mix of independent shops and some high street chains. These are the places to buy jewellery, accessories and international fashion brands. The main shopping street in Newcastle has always been **Northumberland Street** and it remains as popular as ever, especially now it has been pedestrianised.

WHAT TO BUY

There are no particular regional specialities, apart from a few 'Geordie' souvenirs, but the attraction of shopping in Newcastle is the sheer variety of goods available, from basic clothing to designer fashions, stationery to sophisticated electricals and ornaments to household furniture – it is all there.

MARKETS

The main market in Newcastle is the daily indoor **Grainger Market**. The smaller **Bigg Market** takes place every Tuesday, Thursday and Saturday in the street of the same name, while the famous Sunday morning **Quayside Market** boasts 200 stalls lined up along the historic waterfront.

⬤ *Entrance to Monument Mall*

Eating & drinking

In recent years, eating out has become a much more important part of the local culture and, as a result, a multitude of new restaurants have opened up, particularly in areas like the Quayside, but also in other parts of the city. So much so that in a recent poll, conducted by Rough Guides, a night out in NewcastleGateshead was voted the number one British attraction. In 2007, the Eat! NewcastleGateshead festival was launched to celebrate the northeast's dedication to high-quality food throughout the region, in a series of events held during early summer each year. In the past, Newcastle has been known for its drinking culture, but tastes are now much more sophisticated and a bottle of wine is just as likely to be ordered as a bottle of beer. There is a great variety of ethnic cuisine available, from French and Italian to the more exotic Russian, Mongolian, Japanese and Thai. The Quayside, where in recent years there has been an explosion of new restaurants, should have something to satisfy every palate. **Ouseburn** is an up-and-coming area and **Jesmond**, just out of town, also has a very good selection of quality places to eat. Restaurants are generally open at lunchtime from noon till about 14.30, and in the evening from 19.00 till 22.30 or 23.00. Portions are normally quite generous, and many places will be quite happy to serve tap water if you prefer this to the bottled variety. Tipping is up to you – if you receive very good service then it will be appreciated, but it is not necessary. Pubs are normally open till 23.00.

If you are in the mood for a picnic, there are excellent delicatessen counters in the Fenwick department store and

Waitrose, both of which are in Eldon Square. The best place in the city to eat alfresco is in the recently refurbished and pleasant surroundings of **Leazes Park**, the oldest green space in Newcastle (see page 67).

⬤ *The Pitcher and Piano (see page 63), Quayside*

Entertainment

Newcastle is internationally renowned for the quality and quantity of its entertainment and nightlife, and for many years was referred to as a 'party city'. While today the term 'arty' may be preferred to 'party', it is nevertheless an excellent venue for those visitors who want to enjoy the various facilities on offer, whether that is a traditional pub or a sophisticated late-night lounge. Many of these venues are located on the Quayside, but there are also many pubs and clubs throughout the city and in surrounding areas.

The Gate, near Chinatown, is a multilevel complex with bars, some of which stay open till 03.00, cafés, restaurants, a casino and a 12-screen cinema, all of which should ensure a great evening out, even if you don't go anywhere else! If, however, that isn't enough, there are pubs galore (20 in fact) just down the road in the legendary **Bigg Market**, where informality is the order of the night. Seen as upmarket and stylish, the nearby **Central Station** area has several sophisticated bars, while the outlying student suburb of **Jesmond** has a cosmopolitan ambience.

For those who prefer traditional ales, there are many micro-breweries in the area, which produce local beers, some with strange dialect names like Radgie Gadgie and Workie Ticket, which are probably best left untranslated. You could even try a bottle or two of the celebrated Newcastle Brown Ale in the city of its birth; even though it is brewed elsewhere nowadays, aficionados argue it still tastes just as good!

If pubs and clubs are not for you, then there's a great selection of music venues, theatres and art-house cinemas throughout the city, where you can see anything from *film noir* to shows hot from the West End, or even a enjoy a night of stand-up comedy. For up-to-date listings go to
ⓦ www.mynewcastle.net/events

◐ *Entertainment abounds at The Gate!*

Sport & relaxation

SPECTATOR SPORTS

Football

Football is huge in Newcastle and St James' Park, the home of Newcastle United, regularly attracts crowds of between 40,000 and 52,000 people. Over the years the side has featured many famous international players including Malcolm McDonald, Kevin Keegan and Alan Shearer – legendary figures in the city. Stadium tours are available. ⓐ St James' Park ❶ 0844 372 1892 Ⓦ www.nufc.co.uk Ⓝ Metro: St James; Bus: Q2 ❶ Admission charge for tours

Rugby union

Newcastle Falcons' ground is at Kingston Park in the north of the city and has a capacity of 13,000. There are normally tickets available. Many international players have been involved over the years, notably World Cup winner Jonny Wilkinson. ⓐ Kingston Park Stadium, Brunton Road ❶ 0191 214 5588 Ⓦ www.newcastle-falcons.co.uk Ⓝ Metro: Kingston Park

Basketball

Newcastle Eagles Basketball Club are officially the most successful professional sports team in the northeast and, on Fridays between September and May, thousands of fans cheer on their team. The arena is within walking distance of the city centre, near the Redheugh Bridge. ⓐ Newcastle Metro Radio Arena, Arena Way ❶ 0191 245 3880 Ⓦ www.newcastle-eagles.com Ⓝ Metro: Central Station

PARTICIPATION SPORTS

Swimming

Located near the Haymarket, the City Pool is ideal for a relaxing swim, and there are dedicated lanes for those who want to work harder. Gym facilities, a steam room and sauna provide the perfect antidote to a day's sightseeing or shopping.

ⓐ Northumberland Road ☎ 0191 277 1844
ⓦ www.activenewcastle.co.uk ⏰ 08.30–21.30 Mon, 07.30–21.30 Tues–Fri, 08.30–16.30 Sat, closed Sun ⓝ Metro: Haymarket; Bus: Q2 ❶ Admission charge

Walking

Choose from historical urban trails and walks of all lengths that pass through the city's various green spaces.
ⓦ www.activenewcastle.co.uk/walk

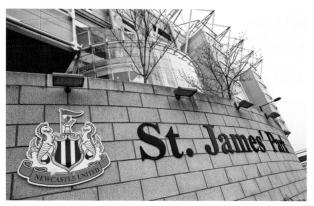

🔺 *Mecca for the 'Toon Army'*

Accommodation

In recent years there has been a huge expansion in the number of rooms available in the city and now there is a full range of accommodation to suit all budgets and needs, from sumptuous 5-star serviced apartments and 4-star hotels through to 1-star guesthouses. Most accommodation tends to be centrally located, either on the Quayside or just outside the centre, but there is also a good selection in the suburb of Jesmond, which is a short Metro ride from the city.

HOTELS & APARTMENTS

The NewcastleGateshead website (ⓦ www.visitnewcastle gateshead.com) has a comprehensive list of hotels and guesthouses, their facilities, locations and links to their websites. There are also self-catering apartments listed, which are a good idea if you wish to stay for more than two or three days. Here are several suggestions which are all in – or within easy travelling distance of – the centre, although there are many more to choose from, especially if you are happy to travel into the city from further afield.

Adelphi Hotel £ Small hotel with comfortable, tastefully decorated rooms, situated in the sought-after, pleasant suburb of Jesmond. ⓐ 63 Fern Avenue, Jesmond ⓣ 0191 281 3109 ⓦ www.adelphihotelnewcastle.co.uk ⓝ Metro: West Jesmond

Bewick Hotel £ Located in Gateshead, about 20 minutes' walk from the Quayside and offering good value for money.

ⓐ 145 Prince Consort Road, Gateshead ⓣ 0191 477 1809
ⓦ www.bewick-hotel.com ⓔ welcome@bewick-hotel.com
ⓝ Metro: Gateshead; Bus: Q1

The Osborne Hotel £ Located in the quiet leafy suburb of
Jesmond (near Jesmond Metro station) yet only 15–20 minutes'
walk from central Newcastle. ⓐ 13–15 Osborne Road, Jesmond
ⓣ 0191 281 3385 ⓦ www.theosbornehotel.co.uk
ⓔ enquiries@theosbornehotel.co.uk ⓝ Metro: Jesmond

Premier Apartments £ (minimum five-night stay)
Contemporary double-bedroom apartments in the heart of
the city. ⓐ Thornton House, Thornton Street ⓣ 0191 279 7900
ⓦ www.premierapartmentsnewcastle.com
ⓔ info@premierapartmentsnewcastle.com ⓝ Metro: Central
Station; Bus: Q1

Angel View Inn ££ Situated in Gateshead overlooking
Antony Gormley's Angel of the North. Fifteen minutes by
car from the city centre. ⓐ Low Eighton Banks, Gateshead
ⓣ 0191 410 3219 ⓦ www.angelviewinn.co.uk
ⓔ reception@angelviewinn.co.uk

Express by Holiday Inn ££ A modern chain hotel in a central
location only 5 minutes' walk from Central Station.
ⓐ Waterloo Square, St James' Boulevard ⓣ 0191 224 6850
ⓦ www.hiexpress.com
ⓔ res.newcastle@expressholiday.inn.co.uk
ⓝ Metro: Central Station; Bus: Q1

Jury's Inn Newcastle ££ Large chain hotel with spacious and comfortable facilities. Public car park adjacent.
ⓐ Scotswood Road ⓣ 191 201 4400 ⓦ www.jurysinns.com
ⓔ jurysinnnewcastle@jurysinns.com ⓝ Metro: Central Station; Bus: Q1

Kensington House ApartHotel ££ Twenty-three serviced apartments, each individually designed and furnished, in the cosmopolitan suburb of Jesmond. ⓐ 5 Osborne Road, Jesmond
ⓣ 0191 281 8175 ⓦ www.kensingtonaparthotel.com
ⓔ stay@kensingtonaparthotel.com ⓝ Metro: Jesmond

Copthorne Hotel £££ Luxury and convenience, with views of the Tyne and its bridges. ⓐ The Close, Quayside
ⓣ 0191 222 0333 ⓦ www.millenniumhotels.com
ⓔ sales.newcastle@millenniumhotels.co.uk ⓝ Metro: Central Station; Bus: Q2

Hilton Newcastle Gateshead £££ Great views of the river and Tyne Bridge and all the luxury you would expect from this international chain only 10-minutes' walk from the centre.
ⓐ Bottle Bank, Gateshead ⓣ 0191 490 9700
ⓦ www.hilton.co.uk/newcastlegateshead ⓝ Metro: Gateshead; Bus: Q1

Malmaison £££ Experience some luxury in this remarkable building on the Quayside. ⓐ Quayside ⓣ 0191 245 5000
ⓦ www.malmaison-newcastle.com
ⓔ newcastle@malmaison.com ⓝ Metro: Central Station; Bus: Q2

93A Grey Street Serviced Apartments £££ (minimum stay two nights) Fully air-conditioned luxury apartments in the heart of Grainger Town. ⓐ 93a Grey Street ⓣ 01661 820 462
ⓦ www.93agreystserviceddapartments.co.uk
ⓔ info@93agreystservicedapartments.co.uk
ⓝ Metro: Monument; Bus Q1, Q2

BED & BREAKFAST

Bed & breakfast accommodation tends to be outside the centre of NewcastleGateshead but is of a high standard.

A1 Summerville Guest House £ Situated in the pleasant village of Whickham and only 10 minutes by car and 20 minutes by bus to Newcastle Centre. ⓐ 33 Orchard Road, Whickham
ⓣ 0191 488 3388 ⓦ www.a1summerville.co.uk
ⓔ info@a1summerville.co.uk

Brandling Guest House £ Opposite a small park in Jesmond but conveniently located for the Haymarket, this comfortable B & B is ideal for a short stay. ⓐ 4 Brandling Park ⓣ 0191 281 3175
ⓦ www.brandlingguesthouse.co.uk ⓝ Metro: Jesmond

YOUTH HOSTEL

Newcastle YHA £ This hostel in a Victorian town house is ideal for visitors on a budget and located in the student quarter of Jesmond. ⓐ 107 Jesmond Road ⓣ 0191 281 2570
ⓦ www.yha.org.uk ⓔ newcastle@yha.org.uk ⓝ Metro: Jesmond

THE BEST OF NEWCASTLE

The centre of Newcastle is quite compact and most of the main sights can be seen comfortably in a couple of days. Stroll along the Quayside, which gives easy access to both sides of the river, and then either walk up Dean Street into Grainger Town or take one of the eco-friendly Quaylink buses, which run regularly between the two areas.

TOP 10 ATTRACTIONS

- **Grey's Monument** Set right in the middle of the city, this tall and elegant structure commemorates Earl Grey, a 19th-century Prime Minister (see page 45).

- **Bessie Surtees House** A Jacobean mansion on the Quayside from which a notorious elopement took place (see pages 55–6).

- **The Sage Gateshead** This magnificent curved-glass structure by the River Tyne is a major music venue (see pages 60–61).

- **Millennium Bridge** The unique bridge across the Tyne for pedestrians and cyclists, often referred to as the 'Blinking Eye' (see page 58).

- **Castle Keep** An impressive medieval structure built to defend the city against marauding Scots (see page 58).

- **BALTIC** A major international centre for contemporary art, having exhibited, among others, Anish Kapoor, Sam Taylor-Wood and Spencer Tunick (see pages 59–60).

- **All Saints Church** This extraordinary elliptical 18th-century church with its splendid spire is a Newcastle landmark (see page 55).

- **Grainger Market** A superb example of a Victorian covered market right in the city centre (see page 45).

- **Discovery Museum** Fantastic science museum includes the first turbine-powered ship, the *Turbinia* (see page 70).

- **Tyne Bridge** This iconic structure across the river, dating from 1928, is for many the symbol of Tyneside (see pages 57–8).

🔻 *Millennium Bridge*

Suggested itineraries

HALF-DAY: NEWCASTLE IN A HURRY

While half a day isn't sufficient to experience Newcastle fully, it will be enough to whet your appetite for a return trip. Go to the Quayside and visit Bessie Surtees House with its Jacobean façade and interesting interior. From the Quayside there is a great view of all the bridges, as well as of BALTIC and The Sage. If you have time, cross the river and have a look inside BALTIC, then catch a bus back to the centre.

1 DAY: TIME TO SEE A LITTLE MORE

If you have a full day to spend in Newcastle, follow the half-day tour recommendation and then have some lunch on the Quayside before you return to the centre. Visit the fascinating Discovery Museum or perhaps the Laing Art Gallery, where you could comfortably spend the rest of the day. You might even have some time left to do a little shopping!

2–3 DAYS: SHORT CITY BREAK

You should be able to see most of Newcastle's main attractions in two or three days. Grainger Town is of great architectural interest, and the Grainger Market and nearby Central Arcade are both worth strolling through; the churches reward a visit too. The Quayside has enough of interest to occupy most of a day, and the remainder of your time could be spent exploring further out of the centre, where the Great North Museum: Hancock, for example, can be found.

LONGER: ENJOYING NEWCASTLE TO THE FULL

If you are fortunate enough to have longer then you will have time to enjoy a couple of long lunches in the centre and further out. More time can also be devoted to appreciating properly the museums and galleries. There will be time too to visit the small town of Alnwick and the city of Durham, which are each worth a day alone.

⬤ *Swirle Pavillion, Quayside*

Something for nothing

In many respects, Newcastle is not a particularly expensive city to visit and it is possible to do a great deal without spending very much. However, it is also possible to have an enjoyable morning or afternoon that will cost absolutely nothing – and if you enjoy a stroll in pleasant surroundings, then so much the better.

A walk along the Quayside is one such free excursion. See the Jacobean façade and wonderful period interior of Bessie Surtees House on Sandhill free of charge, then go down onto the Quayside and take time to enjoy the classical architecture on the Newcastle side, as well as the view of the ultra-modern Sage on the Gateshead Quays. Cross the Millennium Bridge and head for the unmistakable BALTIC Centre, where even if contemporary artwork is not your thing, you can enjoy the view from the top floor – and all for free.

Newcastle's churches, museums and art galleries are also free to look around. In particular don't miss the Discovery Museum, the Great North Museum: Hancock and the Laing Art Gallery.

When it rains

Rain is far from unknown in Newcastle, and downpours can happen at any time of year: make sure you have an umbrella and/or suitable clothing. The good news, however, is that if the weather is wet, there are still plenty of activities to keep you busy while also providing a roof over your head – and some of them are even free as well.

The malls at Eldon Square and Eldon Garden shopping centres are connected, and together provide sufficient shops and cafés to keep even the most committed shopper sated. If that isn't enough, then the Grainger Market and Monument Mall provide shelter too. For a slightly more cultural morning or afternoon protected from the elements, a visit to one of the first-class museums or perhaps the wonderful Laing Art Gallery or BALTIC Centre might fit the bill. A couple of hours' quiet browsing in the Lit & Phil or the City Library may appeal to some visitors, and of course the 12-screen cinema at the Gate offers plenty of films to while away any rainy hours.

On arrival

FINDING YOUR FEET

Geordies are known the world over as friendly and welcoming people, always willing to help visitors to the city of which they are so proud. This, together with the fact that the centre is so compact and easy to find your way around, means that the visitor can feel at home and relaxed straightaway. Relaxation is the key in Newcastle and it is the case that, except in the more sophisticated restaurants, casual clothing is acceptable – and indeed the norm.

Don't allow yourself to get too relaxed, however, because while Newcastle is generally a very safe city, pickpockets do operate, especially in the busy shopping areas. Also, if you are not happy in boisterous crowds, it is probably best to avoid parts of Grainger Town – especially the infamous Bigg Market – and the Quayside, on Friday evenings in particular, when many young people from the surrounding areas pour into the city to enjoy themselves, so you should bear this in mind if you are planning a night out. If there is a serious incident, dial '999' in the usual way, but the police can also be contacted on the following non-emergency number ☎ 03456 043 043. For further information go to ⓦ www.northumbria.police.uk. Apart from the shopping malls, only Northumberland Street in the centre is closed to vehicular traffic, and care needs to be taken when crossing the roads, especially in the area around Grey's Monument, as the traffic often moves very quickly and quietly through this part of the city. It is best to pay heed to the traffic lights and cross the roads in the centre only at designated crossings.

⬤ *Grey's Monument*

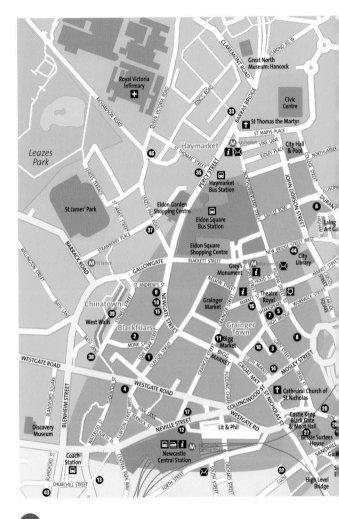

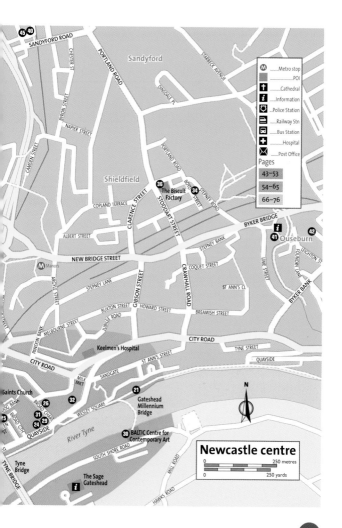

SANDYFORD ROAD
CHESTER ST
PORTLAND ROAD
Sandyford
STARBECK AVENUE
BYRON STREET
NAPIER STREET
DINSDALE PL
CAMDEN STREET
PORTLAND ROAD
BOYD STREET
STENEY ROAD
Shieldfield
The Biscuit Factory
COPLAND TERRACE
CLARENCE STREET
STODDART STREET
ALBERT STREET
BYKER BRIDGE
NEW BRIDGE STREET
Manors
STEPNEY BANK
Ouseburn
LIME STREET
FOUNDRY LANE
LEIGHTON ST
ARGYLE STREET
STEPNEY LANE
GIBSON STREET
CRAWHALL ROAD
COQUET STREET
ST ANN'S CL
BYKER BANK
BUXTON STREET
HOWARD STREET
BREAMISH STREET
JUBILEE ROAD
PANDON BANK
MELBOURNE STREET
CITY ROAD
TYNE STREET
Keelmen's Hospital
ST ANN'S STREET
QUAYSIDE
CITY ROAD
SANDGATE
MILK MKT
Saints Church
Gateshead Millennium Bridge
WESLEY SQUARE
N
DOCK BANK
BROAD CHARE
QUAYSIDE
BROAD CH
BALTIC Centre for Contemporary Art
River Tyne
SOUTH SHORE ROAD
MILL ROAD
Newcastle centre
TYNE BRIDGE
Tyne Bridge
The Sage Gateshead
HAWKS ROAD

Legend:
Ⓜ ....Metro stop
▪ ....POI
✝ ....Cathedral
ℹ ....Information
🛡 ....Police Station
🚉 ....Railway Stn
🚌 ....Bus Station
✚ ....Hospital
✉ ....Post Office

Pages
43–53
54–65
66–76

0 ——— 250 metres
0 ——— 250 yards

ORIENTATION

A good way to orientate yourself is to take an open-top bus tour of the city, which takes in all the major sights, including the BALTIC state-of-the-art centre for contemporary visual arts (see pages 59–60), St James' Park (see pages 67–8), The Sage (see pages 60–61), The Biscuit Factory (see page 69), Gateshead Millennium Bridge (see page 58) and Eldon Square (see page 14). Tours start at the Central Station, last for an hour and can be booked in advance at ⓦ www.city-sightseeing.com. Details are also available from the Tourist Information Centres.

The centrally placed Grey's Monument is a significant landmark in Grainger Town, but is not tall enough to be seen from everywhere and has to be sighted along the streets rather than over the rooftops. From the Monument, Grainger Town begins to slope down more and more steeply in a southerly direction, along Grey Street and then Dean Street towards the river, which runs from west to east between the Newcastle Quays on the north bank and the Gateshead Quays on the south bank. There are several landmarks on the Quayside, including some of the famous bridges, with the High Level at its western end and the Millennium Bridge to its east. The curved-glass structure of The Sage and the striking brick, glass and concrete of BALTIC stand proudly on the Gateshead shore, while on the Newcastle side the Castle Keep and spires of All Saints Church and the Cathedral Church of St Nicholas tower above their surroundings.

The area described as 'Outside the city centre' in this guide forms an arc around Grainger Town, stretching from Scotswood Road in the west through Haymarket in the north all the way to

🔺 *All Saints Church*

the Ouseburn River, at the point at which it flows into the Tyne at the eastern edge of the city. The main landmarks in this area are the unmistakable towering stands of St James' Park football ground, while at the Haymarket the Carillon Tower of the Civic Centre and the spire of the church of St Thomas the Martyr stand tall above the landscape.

GETTING AROUND

It is possible to cover Newcastle on foot due to the relatively small size of the centre, and it takes no more than 30 minutes at a leisurely pace to walk through the city from the Haymarket to the Gateshead Quays or across it from Chinatown to the Ouseburn. In the city itself there are regular and efficient bus services, should you need them, with timetables displayed at each stop, and these, used in conjunction with the Metro system, should satisfy all your transport needs. The eco-friendly hybrid Quaylink buses, the Q1 and the Q2, will take you very close to most of the sights and attractions mentioned in this guide, without the need for any other form of transport. These bright yellow buses run approximately every 10 minutes between 07.00 and 23.00, seven days a week.

Both the towns selected for the 'Out of Town trips', Alnwick and Durham, are easy to reach by bus or car, while the latter is also readily accessible by train from Newcastle Central Station. In the case of Durham, there is also a Park & Ride option. Both of these places have a very small centre and public transport should not be needed, as you can walk to all the sights in a few minutes. The MetroCentre can be reached by train from Newcastle Central Station in about 10 minutes, or by bus

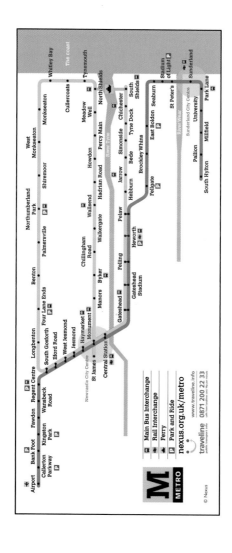

from the Eldon Square Bus Concourse. The beautiful beaches on both sides of the Tyne are easily accessible using the Metro system.

CAR HIRE

If you plan to spend all your time in Newcastle itself, you don't need to hire a car. If, however, you wish to visit some outlying areas, including perhaps Alnwick or Durham, then all the usual car-rental companies can be found in the city. It may even be a good idea to book a car before you arrive, especially at busy times, but if you have been unable to do this then your hotel should be able to help you.

◑ *Newcastle's bridges*

THE CITY OF
Newcastle

Introduction to city areas

For the purposes of this book, Newcastle has been divided up into three areas: **Grainger Town**, the heart of the city, where some of the country's finest neoclassical buildings and streets are to be found; **The Quayside**, a thriving and cosmopolitan area with its bars, restaurants and major architectural landmarks; and **Outside the city centre**, encircling Grainger Town and the Quayside, with parks and green spaces for picnicking, some excellent museums and the Ouseburn Valley, a former heavily industrialised area which has been regenerated into something of a cultural oasis. Within these three areas you will find all of Newcastle's top attractions, from the BALTIC Centre for Contemporary Art to St James' Park, the mecca of the 'Toon Army', Newcastle United's fanatical supporters.

⬤ *'Tyneside Classical' architecture, Grainger Town*

Grainger Town

The geographical centre of Newcastle is now known as Grainger Town, after the architect who designed it. By the turn of the 19th century, the area was in need of regeneration, and Richard Grainger, together with his colleague John Dobson, were given the rebuilding task. Effectively they were to do for Newcastle what Baron Georges Haussmann did later for Paris, although admittedly on a smaller scale! For the purposes of this guide, Eldon Square and lower Northumberland Street have been included in this area; while not actually in Grainger Town, they are adjacent to it. The small and unusual Edwardian Central Arcade, built in 1906, is where an excellent Tourist Information Office can be found.

SIGHTS & ATTRACTIONS

Bigg Market

On the southern edge of Grainger Town can be found the Bigg Market, which has existed since at least the 12th century. Not a large market, as you might think, but quite a small one – 'bigg' is simply a dialect word for a type of barley. ⓐ Bigg Market
Ⓝ Metro: Central Station

Blackfriars

At the western edge of Grainger Town, behind The Gate complex, can be found a 13th-century monastery founded by the 'Black' Friars, situated just inside the city walls. The order was dissolved by Henry VIII in 1539 and the buildings were handed over to the trade guilds and then eventually restored. Nowadays a pleasant interval can be passed looking round the galleries and craft workshops, or eating in the restaurant, said to be the oldest dining room in the country. ⓐ Friar Street

Cathedral Church of St Nicholas

A parish church for most of its life, St Nicholas has been a cathedral since 1882. Since it is not a purpose-built cathedral, the church, constructed at the end of the 12th century, lacks a close and a cloister, but nevertheless there is much of interest to be seen, such as some medieval stained glass and, of course, its crowning glory (literally), the Crown Spire with its superb lantern tower.

◯ *Theatre Royal façade*

ⓐ St Nicholas Churchyard ⓣ 0191 232 1939
ⓦ www.stnicholascathedral.co.uk ⓛ 24 hours Thur–Tues,
midnight–17.30 Wed ⓝ Metro: Central Station

Chinatown

At the northern end of what remains of the city walls can be
found the impressive red and gold Chinatown Arch, which
welcomes visitors to Chinatown. Based largely in Stowell
Street, running parallel with the West Walls, it is home to
many Chinese restaurants and other businesses.
ⓐ Stowell Street ⓝ Metro: Central Station, Monument;
Bus: Q2

Grainger Market

Grade I listed, and a fine example of a covered market, built
to replace the old markets that already existed in the vicinity.
A weigh house can be used by the public and the world's
smallest branch of Marks & Spencer exists in the form of a stall
named 'Marks & Spencer Original Penny Bazaar'! ⓐ Grainger St
ⓛ 09.00–17.00 Mon & Wed, 09.00–17.30 Tues & Thur–Sat
ⓝ Metro: Monument; Bus: Q1, Q2

Grey's Monument

Another Grade I listed structure, 40 m (130 ft) high, with its
statue of Lord Grey atop. It was erected in 1838 to commemorate
the passing of the Great Reform Act in 1832. Lord Grey, a local
man, was Prime Minister at the time; he is also well known for a
particular blend of tea that he favoured. ⓐ Blackett Street
ⓝ Metro: Monument; Bus: Q1, Q2

Grey Street

Voted Britain's finest street by BBC Radio 4 listeners in 2004, Grey Street was built in the 1830s, and runs downhill in a curve towards the river to meet Dean Street. It has such a pleasing aspect that the poet John Betjeman was moved to say: 'As for the curve of Grey Street, I shall never forget seeing it to perfection, traffic-less on a misty Sunday morning. Not even Regent Street, even old Regent Street London, can compare with that descending subtle curve.' ⓐ Grey Street Ⓝ Metro: Monument; Bus: Q1, Q2

West Walls

Just beyond Blackfriars are what is left of the city walls, which were constructed during the 13th and 14th centuries and are now known as the West Walls. ⓐ West Walls Ⓝ Metro: Central Station

CULTURE

Laing Art Gallery

Home to a stunning collection of artworks, in particular some important 18th- and 19th-century paintings and contemporary works. There are also fun activities for families and events for children during the school holidays. ⓐ New Bridge Street ⓣ 0191 232 7734 Ⓦ www.twmuseums.org.uk/laing Ⓛ 10.00–17.00 Mon–Sat, 14.00–17.00 Sun Ⓝ Metro: Monument; Bus: Q2

The Literary & Philosophical Society (The Lit & Phil)

Visitors are welcome to look around and browse the open shelves of this large independent library, founded in 1793. It is located near to the Central Station in a Grade II listed building opened in 1825. The society was founded as a conversation club, although politics and religion were expressly excluded, and was very liberal in its outlook, admitting female members from as early as 1804.

The library rooms have changed little since the early days, and entering them it is easy to imagine being back in the 19th century. Famous members have included the architect Richard Grainger, his colleague John Dobson, Earl Grey, Robert Stephenson and – more recently – Neil Tennant of the Pet Shop Boys. ⓐ 23 Westgate Road ⓦ www.litandphil.org.uk ⓛ 09.30–19.00 Mon, Wed & Thur, 09.30–20.00 Tues, 09.30–17.00 Fri, 09.30–13.00 Sat ⓜ Metro: Central Station

Theatre Royal

A visit to this magnificent theatre in the heart of Grainger Town to take in one of the splendid productions available all year round would be a highlight of any visit to Newcastle. The exquisite Palladian entrance sets the scene for a magnificent interior, where 380 productions – as diverse as Shakespeare (the RSC visits annually), contemporary dance, ballet and pantomime – take place each year. Recently the subject of a £7.2 million refurbishment, it has a new box office, a stage which can now accommodate the most lavish productions and the Caffè Teatro, which offers very tempting fare all day. A further refurbishment of the auditorium during 2011 will restore this to the 1901 design of the gifted Frank Matcham (1854–1920), who also designed the London Coliseum.

Tours of the theatre are available, although these will be slightly restricted during the refurbishment of the auditorium.

Check the website or ring for further details. ⓐ 100 Grey Street
ⓣ 08448 11 21 21 ⓦ www.theatreroyal.co.uk ⓝ Metro: Monument;
Bus: Q1, Q2

RETAIL THERAPY

If you enjoy shopping, then Grainger Town and the Eldon Square
complex are for you. Every conceivable type of shop can be
found here, from the sophistication of John Lewis and Fenwick
to chic boutiques selling the latest fashions, and from tempting
speciality food stores to ubiquitous mobile-phone shops.

Castle Galleries Specialising in limited edition and collectable
art. ⓐ Ground Floor, Monument Mall ⓣ 0191 233 2200
ⓦ www.castlegalleries.com ⓝ Metro: Monument;
Bus: Q1, Q2

Debenhams Recently opened department store specialising in
women's wear and accessories, with a mix of own brands as
well as other labels. ⓐ 26 St Andrew's Way ⓣ 08445 616 161
ⓦ www.debenhams.com ⓝ Metro: Monument; Bus: Q2

Fenwick Department store selling everything from cosmetics
and fashion to electrical goods and furniture on five floors.
ⓐ Northumberland Street ⓣ 0191 232 5100
ⓦ www.fenwick.co.uk ⓝ Metro: Haymarket

John Lewis Fenwick's main rival, John Lewis sells much the same
range of goods on four levels and takes great pride in its level of

customer service. ⓐ Eldon Square ⓣ 0191 232 5000
ⓦ www.johnlewis.com ⓝ Metro: Monument

Neal's Yard Ethical and ecologically sound health and beauty
products. ⓐ Central Arcade ⓣ 0191 232 2525
ⓦ www.nealsyardremedies.com ⓝ Metro: Monument; Bus: Q2

The Pen Shop This writing instrument specialist is now a
national chain, but originated in Newcastle as T & G Allen, the
stationers. ⓐ Eldon Gardens ⓣ 0191 232 3853
ⓦ www.penshop.co.uk ⓝ Metro: Monument; Bus: Q2

Richard Sinton Independent jewellery boutique offering
contemporary pieces by designers such as Paul Spurgeon, and
classical jewellery by Dior, amongst others. ⓐ 47–48 Eldon
Garden ⓣ 0191 232 0788 ⓦ www.richardsintonjewellers.co.uk
ⓝ Metro: Monument; Bus Q2

🔺 *Inside the Grainger Market*

Twenty Five Lifestyle store selling upmarket furniture and household goods by Kosta Boda, Georg Jensen and Smythson. Eldon Garden 0191 231 4062 Metro: Monument; Bus: Q2

Windows Established in 1908, this independent retailer has three floors of music-related products, ranging from guitars and pianos to CDs and sheet music. Central Arcade 0191 232 1356 www.jgwindows.com Metro: Monument; Bus: Q2

TAKING A BREAK

There are numerous places throughout Grainger Town in which to take an enjoyable break from sightseeing or shopping, ranging from the relatively recent phenomenon – in Newcastle at least – of pavement cafés to traditional pubs, or from independent restaurants to those in the department stores.

Bangkok Café £ Based on a typical Bangkok establishment. Eat in or take-away, lots of vegetarian options. 39 Low Friar Street 0191 260 2323 www.atbangkokcafe.co.uk noon–15.00 & 17.30–22.00 Mon–Fri, noon–22.00 Sat & Sun Metro: St James

Blackfriars Café Bar £ This medieval dining room is the oldest in the UK. Monk Street 0191 261 5945 www.blackfriarsrestaurant.co.uk 11.00–17.00 & 18.00–late Mon–Sat, 11.00–16.00 Sun (summer); noon–14.30 & 18.00–late Mon–Sat, noon–16.00 Sun (winter) Metro: Central Station, St James; Bus: Q2

Blakes Coffee House £ ❸ Serving sandwiches and snacks in a lively atmosphere. ⓐ 53 Grey Street ☏ 0191 261 5463 🕐 07.00–18.00 Mon–Fri, 07.30–17.30 Sat, 10.00–16.00 Sun Ⓝ Metro: Monument; Bus: Q1, Q2

The Salsa Café £ ❹ Tapas in a relaxed atmosphere. ⓐ 89–93 Westgate Road ☏ 0191 221 1022 Ⓦ www.salsacafe.com 🕐 11.00–23.00 Mon–Sat, noon–23.00 Sun Ⓝ Metro: Central Station; Bus: Q1

Flatbread Café ££ ❺ Dishes and dips with a North African or Persian theme. ⓐ 69–75 High Bridge Street ☏ 0844 736 6166 (Option 1) Ⓦ www.flatbreadcafe.com 🕐 17.00–21.30 Mon–Wed, 17.00–21.00 Thur, 17.00–23.00 Fri, noon–23.00 Sat Ⓝ Metro: Monument; Bus: Q1, Q2

Grainger Rooms ££ ❻ Simple seasonal local food prepared by a leading chef. ⓐ 7 Higham Place ☏ 0191 232 4949 🕐 11.30–14.30 & 17.30–21.30 Mon–Sat Ⓝ Metro: Monument; Bus: Q2

Pani's ££ ❼ Stylish Italian café offering panini and pasta dishes. ⓐ 61 High Bridge Street ☏ 0191 232 4366 Ⓦ www.paniscafe.co.uk 🕐 10.00–22.00 Mon–Sat, closed Sun Ⓝ Metro: Monument; Bus: Q1, Q2

Secco ££ ❽ Puglian-inspired cuisine in an award-winning three-storey building. ⓐ 86 Pilgrim Street ☏ 0191 230 0444 Ⓦ www.seccouk.com 🕐 noon–14.30 & 17.30–22.30 Mon–Fri, noon–22.30 Sat, closed Sun Ⓝ Metro: Monument; Bus: Q1, Q2

AFTER DARK

Newcastle's nightlife is legendary – here are just a few
highlights.

Aspers at the Gate 9 Casino, spa retreat and live
entertainment. ⓐ The Gate, Newgate Street ⓣ 0191 255 0400
🕒 Casino noon–06.00 daily; Bar 14.00–03.00 daily
Ⓜ Metro: St James, Monument; Bus: Q2

Bar Bannatyne 10 Upmarket bar-restaurant with Moroccan/
Mediterranean styling. ⓐ The Gate, Newgate Street
ⓣ 0191 261 9666 🕒 10.00–01.00 daily Ⓜ Metro: St James; Bus: Q2

Blu Bambu 11 Perhaps Newcastle's most popular nightclub.
ⓐ Bigg Market ⓣ 0191 261 5811 🕒 Thur & Sun 10.00–02.00; Fri &
Sat 10.00–03.00 Ⓜ Metro: Monument; Bus: Q1, Q2

🔺 *Central Arcade*

The Centurion ⓬ Dubbed by the *Observer* as Newcastle's most impressive watering hole. ⓐ Central Station, Neville Street ⓣ 0191 261 6611 ⓛ 10.00–midnight Mon–Sat, 10.00–23.00 Sun ⓝ Metro: Central Station; Bus: Q1

Digital ⓭ Great club nights. ⓐ Times Square ⓣ 0191 261 9755 ⓛ 10.30–02.30 Mon, Tues & Thur, 10.00–03.00 Wed, 10.30–03.30 Fri & Sat, closed Sun ⓝ Metro: Central Station; Bus: Q1

Flares ⓮ 1970s revival bar. ⓐ 31 Mosley Street ⓣ 0191 261 1029 ⓛ 20.00–01.00 Mon–Thur, 20.00–02.00 Fri, 19.30–02.00 Sat ⓝ Metro: Central Station; Bus: Q1

The Keel Row ⓯ Named for the keelmen and their keels (see page 59). ⓐ The Gate, Newgate Street ⓣ 0191 229 9430 ⓛ 10.00–01.00 daily ⓝ Metro: St James, Monument; Bus: Q2

Legends ⓰ An underground rock music club. ⓐ 77 Grey Street ⓣ 0191 232 0430 ⓛ 22.00–03.00 Wed & Fri, 22.00–02.00 Thur, 20.00–03.00 Sat ⓝ Metro: Monument; Bus: Q1, Q2

The Lounge ⓱ Trendy bar near the station. ⓐ 8 Neville Street ⓣ 0191 261 2211 ⓛ 11.00–01.00 Mon–Wed, 11.00–02.00 Thur–Sat, noon–22.30 Sun ⓝ Metro: Central Station; Bus: Q1

The Old George ⓲ One of Newcastle's oldest pubs. ⓐ Cloth Market ⓣ 0191 269 3061 ⓛ 12.00–23.00 Mon–Thur, 11.00–02.00 Fri & Sat, 19.00–22.30 Sun ⓝ Metro: Central Station; Bus: Q1

The Quayside

The Quayside is the area on both banks of the Tyne stretching from the High Level Bridge at its western edge to the Ouseburn valley in the east. For centuries the Quayside was the economic heart of Newcastle, due mainly to the coal industry, when ships bound for London and other centres of population were loaded with coal by the 'keelmen'. Following the reduction in the export of 'Old King Coal' from the river, the area went into decline, but in recent years there has been a rebirth, with much rebuilding, and the Quayside has once again come to the fore.

SIGHTS & ATTRACTIONS

Strolling east along the Quayside, heading towards the **Millennium Bridge**, you will pass several interesting features, including the 19th-century Customs House and the extremely narrow Plummer Chare. Passing under the Tyne Bridge, King Street provides a splendid view of **All Saints Church**; slightly further along is Broad Chare – so called because it allowed two people to walk side by side – flanked on its eastern side by the Law Courts, an impressive, modern red sandstone structure opened in 1990. Further along the Quayside, past Cox Chare, is one of the first reinforced concrete structures in the world, now the Malmaison Hotel. Just in front of the Malmaison can be found a modern, elevated, 10.5 m- (35 ft-) high bust of the Tyne God by Andre Wallace, and in Wesley Square a fascinating Tyne Relief Sculpture by Neil Talbot, which traces on a sandstone wall the course of the River Tyne from Tynemouth to Hexham, about

48 km (30 miles) inland. This side of the river is also home to a range of restaurants and pubs lining the waterfront.

Cross to Gateshead Quays using the amazing Millennium Bridge and admire to your left the impressive structure of the **BALTIC Centre for Contemporary Art** and to your right **The Sage Gateshead** (see pages 59–61). Designed by Lord Foster and Partners, The Sage opened in 2004 as a public performance space.

All Saints Church

All Saints Church was built at the end of the 18th century to an elliptical design by local architect David Stephenson on the foundations of a medieval church. It stands at the top of a flight of stone steps just above the waterfront. The commanding spire, added later, is a Quayside landmark. The church was deconsecrated in the early 1960s but is still in use as an office and auditorium. ⓐ Lower Pilgrim Street ⓣ 0191 267 9222 ⓛ Call to make an appointment

Bessie Surtees House

Jacobean elegance can be found linked to scandalous goings-on in Bessie Surtees House on Sandhill, not far from the granite towers of the Tyne Bridge. The 16th- and 17th-century frontage of the two houses, Surtees House and Milbank House, actually conceals much older buildings, but during the Jacobean period these were wealthy merchants' houses.

Bessie was the daughter of one such very rich merchant, Aubone Surtees. In 1771 Bessie met a young man called John Scott, but her father considered him her social inferior and opposed their relationship. They decided to elope, and the

window from which 17-year-old Bessie climbed down on
18 November 1772 can still be seen. They were able to marry in
Blackshields, Scotland, under Scottish law. The event scandalised
local society, and her father eventually moved out of town to
escape the notoriety of the affair. The irony is that John Scott
later became a rich MP and finally Lord Chancellor of England,
with his wife Bessie destined to become a legendary local figure.
The building is now the North East Regional Office of English
Heritage, and three richly decorated rooms with 17th-century
panelling and distinctive fireplaces can be visited. An exhibition
relating to the history of the house can be seen on the first floor.
ⓐ 41–44 Sandhill ⓣ 0191 269 1200 ⓛ 10.00–16.00 Mon–Fri,
closed 24 Dec–7 Jan and bank holidays ⓝ Bus: Q1, Q2.

⬥ *The iconic Tyne Bridge*

Bridges

The Quayside is really defined by its magnificent bridges, all of which are world-famous structures. There are in fact seven crossings, but the four most interesting are also an essential part of the Quayside. The recently restored **High Level Bridge** is the oldest of the existing structures, designed by the great engineer Robert Stephenson and opened in 1849. It is a dual-purpose, double-deck structure, with the railway running on the upper deck and the road on the lower.

Slightly further downstream is the unusual **Swing Bridge**, opened in 1876 on the site of the old Roman bridge. It was built to replace the Georgian stone bridge which had restricted river traffic and necessitated the use of keels (barges) to bring coal downstream and load up larger vessels well beyond the bridges. The new bridge was built by W G Armstrong, the arms manufacturer, who employed a revolutionary design based on the technology used to rotate the guns on naval ships. This meant that the deck of the bridge could be turned through 90 degrees, allowing large vessels to pass. Subsequently this enabled Armstrong to build naval ships at Elswick, further upstream. Still in use today, and swinging to allow the occasional pleasure craft through, it provides an important road crossing between Newcastle and Gateshead.

Perhaps the most iconic bridge of all is the majestic **Tyne Bridge**, built high above the Quayside, which was the first single-span arch bridge in the UK. It was opened in 1928 by King George V and provided a vital road link, which until the 1990s was the A1 or Great North Road to Scotland from London. Now repainted in its original green, the bridge is a symbol of the region's industrial past and is held in great affection by Geordies everywhere.

Arguably the most graceful structure of all is also the most recent: the **Gateshead Millennium Bridge** opened in September 2001 and is for pedestrians and cyclists only. It has helped considerably in the revitalisation of the Quayside, allowing easy access to The Sage Gateshead and BALTIC. Often referred to as the 'Blinking Eye' it features a unique tilting mechanism to allow ships through. The whole assemblage rotates, and as the arch tilts lower the pathway rises, creating a counterbalance that saves energy. Visitors can watch the bridge opening and a timetable is posted at each end of the structure.

Castle Keep

This impressive fortress is situated at the northern approach to the High Level Bridge. It is easy to see why this was such a strategic position in the Middle Ages. It was constructed between 1168 and 1178, during the reign of Henry II, on the site of an earlier wooden castle. However, by the time the town walls were constructed in the mid-14th century, it had ceased to have any military significance, and in 1589 was described as a ruin. Several restorations have resulted in a structure well worth visiting. An interesting museum can be found on the second floor and the roof space affords fabulous views of the river and bridges. A Grade 1 listed building and a Scheduled Ancient Monument, it stands majestically above the Quayside. ⓐ Castle Keep, Castle Garth ⓦ www.castlekeep-newcastle.org.uk ⓛ 10.00–17.00 Mon–Sat, noon–17.00 Sun (last admission 16.15) ⓝ Bus: Q1, Q2 ⓘ Admission charge

Keelmen's Hospital

The keelmen were a group of highly skilled workers, unique to the northeast, who used 'keels' or barges with a very shallow draught to take coal to the larger, ocean-going vessels which could not negotiate the higher reaches of the river. These colourful characters wore blue jackets, yellow waistcoats, bell-bottom trousers and silk hats with ribbons; they were said to originate in the Scottish borders and settled in Sandgate in medieval times. Despite being very tough, resilient and independent men, their work was so demanding that they could rarely continue to work beyond their mid-forties, so in 1701 the hospital was established to look after sick and elderly keelmen and their families. There are no longer any keelmen, but they are still fondly remembered in the Tyneside song, 'Weel [Well] May The Keel Row'. ⓐ City Road ❶ Closed to the public

CULTURE

BALTIC Centre for Contemporary Art

This landmark industrial building was built in 1950s as a grain warehouse. Only the north and south façades were retained during the reconstruction, however, and six main floors and three mezzanines were placed between the façades, creating in effect a new internal structure, which opened to the public in July 2002.

BALTIC offers the visitor a continually changing programme of contemporary art from around the world. There are no permanent exhibitions and the work on display utilises an astonishing 3,000 sq m (32,290 sq ft) of space, divided into four galleries and a flexible performance area. A bookshop and café on the ground floor, a rooftop restaurant and viewing platform on Level 6 all add to the experience. ⓐ South Shore Road, Gateshead Quays ⓣ 0191 478 1810 ⓦ www.balticmill.com ⓛ 09.30–17.30 Sat–Thur, 09.30– 17.00 Fri ⓝ Bus: Q1

The Sage Gateshead
Another unique landmark, this contemporary structure is fascinating to observe and to explore. Designed by Lord Foster and Partners, it is both a venue for live musical performances of

ⓐ *The stainless steel and glass curves of The Sage*

all genres and a centre for music education. Opened in 2004, the public performance space consists of two performance halls – Halls One and Two, which offer first-class acoustics – as well as the Northern Rock Foundation Hall for rehearsal and performance, and a Music Education Centre consisting of 25 rooms. The spaces are covered by a revolutionary, shell-like structure that is in the form of a triple wave. Fully glazed façades to the east and west, and large glazed apertures in the shell facing the river, give magnificent views.

The concert programme featuring regional, national and international music extends throughout the year; this is also an exceptionally well-equipped venue for local performers. Tours are available. ⓐ St Mary's Square, Gateshead Quays ⓘ 0191 443 4666 (reception); 0191 443 4661 (ticket office) ⓦ www.thesagegateshead.org ⓛ 09.00–21.00 daily (later in summer) Ⓝ Bus: Q2

RETAIL THERAPY

In terms of retail therapy, the Quayside is best known for its Sunday Market, when numerous stalls line the Newcastle Quay. There are also some specialist art and photography galleries selling merchandise.

Lazarides This recently opened gallery exhibits and sells contemporary art, featuring work by Banksy and Jamie Hewlett amongst others. ⓐ Eldon Chambers, 77A Quayside ⓘ 0191 221 2560 ⓦ www.lazinc.com ⓛ 11.00–19.00 Mon–Fri, 11.00–18.00 Sat, 11.00–16.00 Sun Ⓝ Bus: Q2

Side Gallery Amber, the film and photography collective, hold exhibitions and also sell books, dvds and photographs from this gallery. A 48-seat cinema on the premises shows films on Tuesday evenings. 🅐 9 The Side 🕐 0191 232 2000 🅦 www.amber-online.com 🅝 Metro: Central Station; Bus: Q1, Q2

Sunday Market More than 80 stalls line the Quayside every Sunday from 09.30–16.00, as they have done since at least 1736, selling everything from fashion and food to local crafts and toys. 🅦 www.newcastle.gov.uk 🅝 Metro: Central Station; Bus: Q2

TAKING A BREAK

The Quayside is the ideal place to chill out. Take a break and enjoy the scenery and perhaps even do a little bit of people-watching into the bargain. There is an excellent selection of places overlooking the river, or tucked away in quiet side streets – ideal venues in which to spend a relaxing hour or so.

Bob Trollop £ 🔟 Award-winning vegetarian selection served all day in this traditional bar-restaurant. 🅐 32–40 Sandhill 🕐 0191 261 1037 🕒 11.00–midnight Sun–Wed, 11.00–01.00 Thur–Sat 🅝 Metro: Central Station; Bus: Q1, Q2

El Torero £ 🔟 Home-cooked Spanish tapas and paellas. 🅐 Milburn House, The Side 🕐 0191 233 1122 🅦 www.eltorero.co.uk 🕒 noon–23.00 Mon–Sat, noon–22.30 Sun 🅝 Metro: Central Station; Bus: Q1, Q2

Pitcher and Piano £ ㉑ Amazing views of the Quayside from the roof terrace. ⓐ 108 The Quayside ⓣ 0191 232 4110 ⓦ www.pitcherandpiano.com ⓝ Metro: Central Station; Bus: Q1, Q2

Orchid ££ ㉒ New Chinese restaurant opposite the Copthorne Hotel. ⓐ Old Bonded Warehouse, The Close ⓣ 0191 221 1388 ⓛ 17.30–23.00 daily & also noon–14.00 Thur–Sat ⓝ Metro: Central Station; Bus: Q1, Q2

Pan Haggerty ££ ㉓ Named after a delicious local speciality made with potatoes, cheese and onions – try it! ⓐ 21 Queen Street ⓣ 0191 221 0904 ⓦ www.panhaggerty.com ⓛ noon–14.30 & 17.30–21.30 Mon–Fri, noon–14.30 & 18.30–22.00 Sat, noon–16.00 Sun ⓝ Metro: Central Station; Bus: Q1, Q2

Risi's Ices and Gelato Caffè Bar ££ ㉔ Enjoy fantastic views of the Quayside with your ice cream or coffee. ⓐ 31 Quayside 07.00–16.00 daily ⓣ 0191 260 3355 ⓝ Metro: Central Station; Bus : Q1, Q2

Vujon ££ ㉕ Renowned for its original Indian cuisine. ⓐ 29 Queen Street ⓣ 0191 221 0601 ⓦ www.vujon.com ⓛ noon–14.30 & 18.00–23.30 Mon–Sat, closed Sun ⓝ Metro: Central Station; Bus: Q1, Q2

Café 21 £££ ㉖ Award-winning chef Terry Leybourne runs this smart, but not stuffy, restaurant. ⓐ Trinity Gardens ⓣ 0191 222 0755 ⓦ www.cafetwentyone.co.uk ⓛ noon–14.00 & 17.30–22.30 Mon–Sat, 12.30–15.30 & 18.30–22.00 Sun ⓝ Metro: Manors; Bus: Q1, Q2

AFTER DARK

The Quayside is extremely popular after dark, and in recent years there has been a proliferation of new bars and pubs, especially on the Newcastle side of the river.

The Bridge Hotel ㉗ Traditional pub with views of the Quayside next to the High Level Bridge. ⓐ Castle Square ⓣ 0191 232 6400 ⓛ 11.30–23.00 Mon–Thur, 11.30–midnight Fri & Sat, noon–22.30 Sun Ⓝ Metro: Central Station; Bus: Q1, Q2

The Crown Posada ㉘ Probably Newcastle's most famous pub, located in a Grade II listed building. ⓐ 31–33 The Side ⓣ 0191 232 1269 ⓛ noon–23.00 Mon–Wed, 11.00–23.00 Thur, 11.00–midnight Fri, noon–midnight Sat, 19.00–22.30 Sun Ⓝ Metro: Central Station; Bus: Q1, Q2

The Eye on the Tyne ㉙ A sophisticated popular modern bar. ⓐ 11–17 Broad Chare ⓣ 0191 261 7385 ⓛ 11.00–23.00 Sun–Thur, 11.00–midnight Fri & Sat Ⓝ Metro: Central Station; Bus: Q1, Q2

The Riverside Café Bar ㉚ On the ground floor of BALTIC. ⓣ 0191 440 4949 ⓛ 09.00–23.00 Mon–Sat, 09.00–22.30 Sun Ⓝ Metro: Central Station; Bus: Q1, Q2

The Slug and Lettuce ㉛ Vegetarian food available in this upmarket pub overlooking the Tyne. ⓐ Exchange Buildings, Quayside. ⓣ 0191 261 7196 ⓛ 10.00–23.00 Mon–Thur & Sun, 10.00–01.00 Fri & Sat Ⓝ Metro: Central Station; Bus: Q1, Q2

The Waterline ⓐ A large, popular pub close to the Law Courts. Serves pizzas from a clay oven. ⓐ Quayside ⓣ 0191 230 5531 ⓛ noon–23.00 Mon–Sat, noon–22.30 Sun ⓝ Metro: Central Station; Bus: Q1, Q2

◔ BALTIC Centre for Contemporary Art (see page 59)

Outside the city centre

This section includes all the areas that surround the Quayside and Grainger Town on the north side of the river, such as **Ouseburn** in the east, **Gallowgate** (the area around St James' Park) and the **Haymarket** on the northern edge of the city.

Since Newcastle is so compact, it is possible to reach most of these on foot, but for the footsore the excellent public transport system serves them all. Essentially 'Outside the city centre' forms an arc around Grainger Town.

SIGHTS & ATTRACTIONS

City Hall

Opened in 1927, City Hall still retains the atmosphere of a bygone era with its 1920s charm and remarkable architecture. The hall has played host to artists as diverse as Yehudi Menuhin, The Beatles, local lads The Animals, Bruce Springsteen and Elton John; more recently Snow Patrol and Ricky Gervais have provided top billing. ⓐ Northumberland Rd ⓣ 0191 261 2606 ⓜ Metro: Haymarket; Bus: Q2

Civic Centre

Built in the 1960s, the then cutting-edge design of the Civic Centre remains striking. The splendid Carillon Tower with its 25 bells, and the nine gigantic flambeaux at the building entrance, are a deliberate nod to the days when councillors would be summoned to meetings by the town crier pealing his bell and barrels of tar being lit outside. There is also a

magnificent bronze statue of the Tyne God. ⓐ Barras Bridge
ⓣ 0191 277 7222 ⓔ enquiries@thecivicentre.co.uk
ⓝ Metro: Haymarket; Bus: Q2

Leazes Park

The oldest green space in the city, Leazes Park has recently been
restored using the original plans. Extensive planting and the
reintroduction of new ornate gateways have been accompanied
by the restoration of the lake. Rowing boats are available for hire
at weekends and there's a refreshment kiosk. ⓐ Richardson Rd
ⓣ 0191 261 7231 ⓝ Metro: Haymarket

Ouseburn

The area to the east of the City Centre is walkable from the
centre but it may be a good idea to use the Q2 and get off at
Lime Street or one of the nearby stops. These are the lower
reaches of the Ouseburn River, which flows right through the
city before entering an underground culvert, finally emerging
under Byker Bridge and flowing into the Tyne. This is an area
that attracts creative people and there are several cooperatives,
including **The Biscuit Factory** (see page 69), which can be
visited and where contemporary art can be bought. ⓝ Bus: Q2

St James' Park

The wide St James' Boulevard leads to the home of Newcastle
United Football Club, just above Gallowgate. While many would
argue that the structure is not totally in keeping with the
surrounding architecture, it is nevertheless a striking edifice,
with its 52,200 seating capacity. Stadium tours can be booked

on ☎ 0844 372 1892. ⓐ St James' Park ☎ 0191 201 8400
Ⓝ Metro: St James

St Thomas the Martyr

Just east of Leazes Park lies the **Haymarket**, which is home to
the fine 19th-century church of St Thomas the Martyr. This is a
Newcastle landmark, designed in Gothic style by John Dobson.
The building, completed in 1830, replaced a medieval chapel of
the same name that was located near the river. This earlier
building was founded, so the story goes, by one of the assassins
of Thomas Becket, in atonement for his sin. ⓐ Haymarket
☎ 0191 525 1881 Ⓝ Metro: Haymarket; Bus: Q2

⬤ Gothic stylings of St Thomas the Martyr

CULTURE

The Biscuit Factory

One of several galleries in the Ouseburn area, the Biscuit Factory is the largest commercial gallery in the UK, with 3,252 sq m (35,000 sq ft) of floor space on two floors. Artists, photographers, sculptors, ceramists and jewellers all display and sell their work in this fun, relaxed environment. A café and restaurant run by an award-winning chef are also located on the premises. ⓐ 16 Stoddart Street ⓣ 0191 261 1103 ⓦ www.thebiscuitfactory.com ⓛ 11.00–17.00 Sun & Mon, 10.00–18.00 Tues, Wed, Fri & Sat, 10.00–20.00 Thur ⓜ Metro: Manors

City Library

This new state-of-the-art City Library, also called the Charles Avison Building, opened in 2009, and replaced an ugly 1960s structure with an impressive six-storey building and 'glass box' east side, a marble-floored atrium, performance and exhibition spaces and a café. Wi-fi throughout facilitates research, and music can be downloaded from nine stations. For young children there is 'story time' from 14.00–14.30 on Wednesday, Saturday and Sunday. The sixth floor is given over to the permanent Newcastle Collection, and of particular interest is the work of local artist and engraver, the internationally renowned Thomas Bewick. ⓐ Charles Avison Building, 33 New Bridge Street West ⓣ 0191 2774100 ⓦ www.newcastle.gov.uk/newcastlecollection ⓛ 08.30–20.00 Mon–Thur, 08.30–17.30 Fri & Sat, 11.00–17.00 Sun ⓜ Metro: Monument; Bus: Q2

Discovery Museum

This fascinating museum is located in Blandford House, which was built for the Co-operative Wholesale Society as its regional headquarters. Taken over by Tyne & Wear Museums in the 1970s, it was launched as the Discovery Museum in 1993 to highlight the region's shipbuilding heritage and local inventions that changed the world. The entrance hall contains perhaps the most fascinating of these, the *Turbinia*, a 35 m- (115 ft-) long vessel built for naval use by Charles Parsons, which was the first ship in the world to be powered by steam turbine – and the fastest at the time. This is a really fun museum with games and interactive displays for young children located on several levels. ⓐ Blandford Square ⓣ 0191 222 2614 ⓦ www.twmuseums.org.uk/discovery ⓛ 10.00–17.00 Mon–Sat, 14.00–17.00 Sun ⓝ Metro: Central Station

Great North Museum: Hancock

Known for generations simply as 'The Hancock', this impressive stone structure has recently been reopened following a £26million refurbishment programme. It combines the collections of the old Hancock Museum, the Museum of Antiquities, the Shefton Museum and the Hatton Gallery. Perhaps best known for its lifesize T. rex dinosaur skeleton, its Egyptian mummies and planetarium, there are many other fascinating interactive displays, including a large-scale model of Hadrian's Wall – a great family day out. ⓐ Barras Bridge ⓦ www.twmuseums.org.uk/greatnorthmuseum ⓛ 10.00–17.00 Mon–Sat, 14.00–17.00 Sun ⓝ Metro: Haymarket; Bus: Q2

Laing Art Gallery

Founded in 1901 by the philanthropist Alexander Laing, the art gallery has a large permanent collection including the impressive landscapes of John Martin, featuring his *Destruction of Sodom and Gomorrah*, the Pre-Raphaelite William Holman Hunt's *Isabella and the Pot of Basil* and sculptures by Henry Moore, all exhibited in spacious galleries to great effect. Under-fives are also catered for, with a fun play area that helps them learn more about art by dressing up, playing games and solving puzzles.

ⓐ New Bridge Street ⓦ www.twmuseums.org.uk/laing ⓛ 10.00–17.00 Mon–Sat, 14.00–17.00 Sun ⓜ Metro: Monument; Bus: Q2

🔺 *The Hancock has undergone a major refurbishment*

RETAIL THERAPY

The majority of the shops are in Grainger Town; however, there are a few interesting retail outlets in the area.

Armstrong Bridge Market Held every Sunday on the old bridge over Jesmond Dene, now closed to vehicles, this interesting market has many stalls selling locally produced crafts, artwork and leather goods. ⓐ Armstrong Bridge ⓛ 10.00–16.00 Sun

Blackwell Bookshop Serving the nearby universities with a wide range of academic and specialist books as well as fiction and travel. ⓐ 141 Percy Street ⓣ 0191 232 6421 ⓦ www.bookshop.blackwell.co.uk ⓝ Metro: Haymarket; Bus: Q2

Elula New Age shop and coffee bar offering jewellery, incense, candles and gift items such as birth stones. ⓐ 13 Ridley Place ⓣ 0191 261 6128 ⓛ 10.00–17.00 Mon–Sat ⓝ Metro: Haymarket; Bus: Q2

TAKING A BREAK

Perhaps the best way of taking a break outside the centre is, weather permitting, to have a picnic – either in the quiet and picturesque surroundings of Leazes Park, or perhaps in Exhibition Park (just north of the Haymarket). Alternatively try:

Campus Coffee £ ⓲ Run by Newcastle University, this coffee shop and snack bar offers great value and Fairtrade coffee.

ⓐ Kings Walk, Percy Street ⓣ 0191 230 4391 ⓛ 08.00–20.00 daily
ⓝ Metro: Haymarket; Bus: Q2

La Gabbia £ ㉞ Superb cuisine influenced by the different regions of Italy. There is the option to bring your own bottle.
ⓐ Boyd Street, Ouseburn ⓣ 0191 232 6666 ⓛ noon–14.00 & 17.30–21.30 Tues–Sat, 13.00–18.00 Sun ⓝ Metro: Manors; Bus: Q2, 21/22 Central Station

Mark Toney £ ㉟ Established in 1902 and still run by the Mercantonio family, this locally famous ice cream parlour also serves sorbets, sandwiches and even pizza. ⓐ 91 Percy Street ⓣ 0191 266 1879 ⓦ www.marktoney.co.uk ⓛ 07.30–20.00 Mon–Sat, 10.00–20.00 Sun ⓝ Metro: Haymarket; Bus: Q2

🔺 *While away a few hours with the Laing's impressive collection*

Brasserie Black Door ££ Enjoy classic dishes prepared using locally sourced produce. ⓐ The Biscuit Factory, 16 Stoddart Street ⓣ 0191 260 5411 ⓦ www.blackdoorgroup.co.uk
ⓛ noon–14.00 & 19.00–22.00 Mon–Sat, noon–15.00 Sun
ⓜ Metro: Manors

El Coto ££ Arguably the best tapas restaurant in town.
ⓐ 21 Leazes Park Road ⓣ 0191 261 0555 ⓦ www.elcoto.co.uk
ⓛ noon–23.00 daily ⓜ Metro: St James; Bus: Q2

Hanahana ££ Experience teppanyaki cuisine with chefs wearing traditional robes. ⓐ 45 Bath Lane ⓣ 0191 222 0282

⬤ *The Biscuit Factory houses Brasserie Black Door*

🕒 noon–14.00 & 18.00–23.00 Mon–Sat, noon–14.00 & 18.00–22.00 Sun Ⓝ Metro: St James

King Neptune ££ ㊴ If you prefer Pekingese and Szechuan food, then this is the place for you. ⓐ 34–36 Stowell Street
📞 0191 261 6657 🕒 noon–13.45 daily, 18.00–22.45 Mon–Fri, 17.30–23.00 Sat, 18.00–22.30 Sun Ⓝ Metro: St James

AFTER DARK

Outside the centre there is a good choice of venues, especially in Jesmond (particularly around the student quarter of Osborne Road) and in the up-and-coming area of Ouseburn, ranging from traditional pubs to quite sophisticated bars and clubs.

As You Like It ㊵ Bar-restaurant which also puts on music and fashion events. Opposite Mr Lynch (see below). ⓐ Archbold Terrace 📞 0191 281 2277 🌐 www.asyoulikeitjesmond.com
🕒 noon–midnight Sun–Thur, noon–02.00 Fri & Sat
Ⓝ Metro: Jesmond

The Cluny ㊶ Traditional pub and live music venue located in trendy Ouseburn. ⓐ 36 Lime Street, Ouseburn 📞 0191 230 4474
🌐 www.theheadofsteam.com 🕒 11.30–23.00 Mon–Wed, 11.30–midnight Thur, 11.30–01.00 Fri & Sat, noon–22.30 Sun
Ⓝ Metro: Byker, Manors; Bus: 21, 22, 34, 35 Central Station

The Cumberland Arms ㊷ Real ale, cider and live music in this traditional pub. ⓐ James Place Street, Ouseburn 📞 0191 265 6151

www.thecumberlandarms.co.uk 16.00–23.00 Mon, 12.00–23.00 Tues, Thur & Sun, noon–midnight Wed, Fri & Sat
Metro: Byker, Manors; Bus: 21, 22 Central Station

Grosvenor Casino Modern venue with all the usual games, together with a bar and restaurant. 100 St James Boulevard
0191 260 3303 www.grosvenorcasinos.com 24 hours
Metro: Central Station

Liquid & Envy £4 million super-club with state-of-the-art sound and lighting systems as well as 360-degree visual screens.
49 New Bridge Street West 0191 261 2526
22.30–03.00 Mon, Thur, Fri & Sat, closed Tues, Wed & Sun
Metro: Monument; Bus: Q2

Mr Lynch Trendy bar/gastropub with live music at weekends.
Archbold Terrace 0191 281 3810 www.mrlynch.co.uk
noon–02.00 daily Metro: Jesmond

The Trent House Small, friendly corner pub with a soul theme and a 'world famous' (!) jukebox. 1–2 Leazes Lane
0191 261 2154 www.thetrenthouse.co.uk noon–23.00
Mon–Sat, noon–22.30 Sun Metro: Haymarket

The Angel of the North

OUT OF TOWN
trips

Alnwick

Alnwick (pronounced *Annick*) was an important border town in the Middle Ages and two Scottish kings were defeated in battle here, in 1093 and 1174 respectively. From 1309 the castle became the seat of the Percy family, later created earls, then dukes, of Northumberland, who have governed here more or less benevolently ever since. The present duke is still a Percy; his wife, the duchess, initiated the establishment of **The Alnwick Garden**. Even more famous than the duchess is another 'resident' of the castle who, albeit fictional, has achieved worldwide fame as a wizard: the *Harry Potter* movies are filmed here.

The **Tourist Office** is in the Market Place. ⓐ 2, The Shambles ⓣ 01665 511 333 ⓛ 09.00–17.00 Mon–Sat, 10.00–16.00 Sun (restricted hours in winter)

GETTING THERE

Alnwick is 56 km (35 miles) north of Newcastle via the A1 trunk road, and there is adequate parking for cars near the centre. There is no train link, but there are regular Arriva bus services (501 or 505) from Newcastle Haymarket Bus Station.

SIGHTS & ATTRACTIONS

The cobbled market place has always been the hub of this small town, complete with its medieval market cross. It is the best place to start exploring Alnwick.

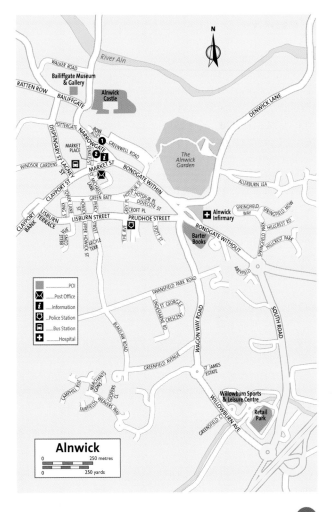

Alnwick

0   250 metres

0   250 yards

Alnwick Castle

Many people come here to see the famous castle, and these numbers have increased significantly since it has featured as Hogwarts School of Witchcraft and Wizardry in the *Harry Potter* films. It is no surprise that the castle is frequently chosen as a film location. It is a striking building, which has been home to the Percy family since 1309. Much of the building is medieval and the Abbot's Tower, the Middle Gateway and the Constable's Tower survive from this time. The curious figures standing on the battlements at first appear medieval too, but were in fact commissioned by the first duke during the restoration he carried out during the late 18th century. The landscaping was carried out under Lancelot 'Capability' Brown. There are guided tours, and plenty of child-friendly activities, including archery lessons and Harry Potter-themed events.

ⓐ Alnwick Castle ⓣ 01665 510 777 ⓦ www.alnwickcastle.com
ⓛ Grounds: 10.00–18.00 daily; State rooms: 10.00–17.00 daily; Knights Quest: 10.00–17.00 daily (31 Mar–29 Oct)
ⓘ Admission charge

The Alnwick Garden

On entering the garden you will be confronted with its magnificent centrepiece, the Grand Cascade, a mass of water tumbling down a slope with a series of 21 weirs set out in Italianate style. Jets of water shoot into the air every 30 minutes, much to the delight of visiting children. Children are also fascinated by the Poison Garden where, under strict supervision, a guide introduces visitors to the various poisonous plants common to both our gardens and the countryside.

Ⓐ Alnwick Castle ⓣ 01665 510 777 Ⓦ www.alnwickgarden.com
🕒 10.00–18.00 daily Apr–Oct; 10.00–16.00 daily Nov–Mar
ⓘ Admission charge

CULTURE

Bailiffgate Museum & Gallery
Presents a fascinating history of the town and the surrounding
area. Ⓐ 14 Bailiffgate ⓣ 01665 605 847
Ⓦ www.bailiffgatemuseum.co.uk 🕒 10.00–17.00 daily Easter–
Oct; 11.00–16.00 daily Nov–Easter ⓘ Admission charge

🔺 *Alnwick Castle*

Barter Books

This destination emporium is located in the disused Victorian railway station and is now one of the largest secondhand bookshops in Britain. ⓐ Alnwick Station ⓣ 01665 604 888 ⓦ www.barterbooks.co.uk ⓛ 09.00–19.00 daily (Apr–Sept); 09.00–17.00 Mon–Sat, 09.00–19.00 Sun (Oct–Mar)

TAKING A BREAK

There are several places in and around Alnwick to take a break, including several pubs and cafés. ⓦ www.visitalnwick.org.uk

Grannie's Delicatessen and Tea Room £ ❶ A cellar restaurant open during the daytime, serving only freshly prepared food. It is popular with locals and visitors alike. ⓐ Narrowgate ⓣ 01665 602 394 ⓛ 09.00–17.00 Mon–Sat, 10.30–16.00 Sun

Lilburns Bar Restaurant ££ ❷ A family-run, modern-style bistro in the centre of town. Its varied menu uses locally sourced food. ⓐ 7 Paikes Street ⓣ 01665 603 444 ⓦ www.lilburns.co.uk ⓛ 10.00–21.00 Tues–Sat, 10.00–17.00 Mon, closed Sun

Durham

Durham, perched high on a peninsular formed by a tight bend in the River Wear, with its magnificent cathedral and castle, is a sight to behold. Durham was founded in AD 995 by monks looking for a safe resting place for the body of St Cuthbert. Legend has it that the saint appeared in a dream and told them to take the coffin to 'Dunholm'. St Cuthbert's tomb can be found at the east end of the cathedral.

After 1066, the Normans appointed prince-bishops who governed the north from Durham for many years. A place of pilgrimage, Durham also became an important university town and, of course, was at the centre of the local coal industry.

GETTING THERE

Durham is 29 km (18 miles) south of Newcastle via the A1 and A1(M). There are car parks in the city and also a Park and Ride System (ⓦ www.durham.gov.uk). By rail it takes less than 20 minutes from Newcastle Central Station and services are very regular. The X2 Arriva bus departs from Eldon Square Bus Concourse and takes approximately one hour to reach Durham.

SIGHTS & ATTRACTIONS

The **Tourist Office** is next to the Gala Theatre. ⓐ 2 Millenium Place ⓣ 0191 384 3720 ⓛ 09.30–17.30 Mon–Sat, 11.00–16.00 Sun. For further information go to ⓦ www.thisisdurham.com

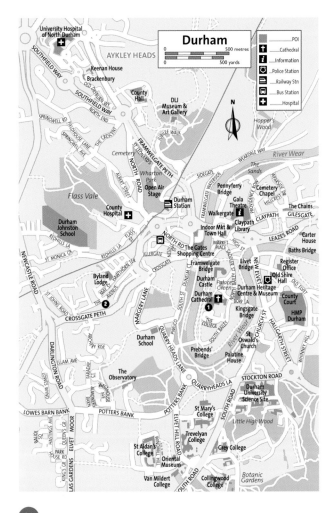

Durham Cathedral

The magnificent castle and cathedral are best viewed together from the pedestrianised old Framwellgate Bridge, while some of the best views of the cathedral itself are from the footpath along the West Bank of the river. The cathedral, constructed between 1093 and 1133, is widely thought to be the best example of Romanesque church architecture in Europe. It has been designated a UNESCO World Heritage Site.

On entering the cathedral by the North Porch door, the visitor is confronted with a large bronze sanctuary knocker, which is in fact a replica, as the real one is exhibited inside. In medieval times, if a citizen seeking sanctuary could reach the knocker, they would be taken into the cathedral. Once inside, stand at the west end of the Nave and imagine how awestruck a medieval worshipper would be when confronted with the sheer size and beauty of the interior. ⓦ www.durhamcathedral.co.uk ⏱ 09.30–18.00 Mon–Sat, 12.30–17.30 Sun (until 20.00 mid-July–Aug); Library: 10.00–13.00 & 14.00–17.00 Mon–Fri

Durham Castle

The original castle was built on the orders of William the Conqueror in the 11th century but successive bishops have restored or altered the building. Like Durham Cathedral, it has been designated a UNESCO World Heritage Site. The castle was the base for the powerful prince-bishops of Durham for centuries. After the founding of Durham University in 1832, the castle was handed over to the new establishment, and today some fortunate students have rooms in the keep. The castle can only be seen on a guided tour, which includes sights such as the

Great Hall, Norman Chapel and a medieval kitchen. ⓐ Palace Green ☎ 0191 334 3800 ⓦ www.dur.ac.uk/university.college ⏰ Guided tours at: 14.00, 15.00, 16.00 Mon–Fri (school term); 10.00, 11.00, noon, 14.00, 15.00, 16.00, 17.00 (school holidays) ⓘ Admission charge

Market Place

With its Victorian **Town Hall, Indoor Market** and statue of the Marquis of Londonderry, who owned much of the coalfield surrounding the city, the Market Place is the hub of Durham.

CULTURE

Durham Heritage Centre & Museum

The story of Durham from medieval times to the modern era is told using interactive displays in a deconsecrated church near the cathedral. ⓐ St Mary-le-Bow, North Bailey ☎ 0191 384 5589 ⓦ www.durhamheritagecentre.org.uk ⏰ 14.00–16.30 Sat–Mon (Easter); 14.00–16.30 weekends and bank holidays (Apr, May & Oct); 14.00–16.30 daily (June); 11.00–16.30 daily (July–Sept) ⓘ Admission charge

RETAIL THERAPY

Durham is not a major shopping centre but there are some good independent shops, an interesting indoor market, and two shopping centres: **The Gates** (indoor) on Framwellgate Bridge and **Prince Bishops**, just off the Market Place. ⏰ 09.00–17.30 Mon–Sat, 11.00–17.00 Sun

Durham Indoor Market A charming Victorian market, established in 1851, with over 50 independent traders.
ⓐ Market Place ⓣ 0191 384 6153 ⓦ www.durhammarkets.co.uk
ⓛ 09.00–17.00 Mon–Sat

Labeado Beads Moroccan beads, bangles and bracelets here to suit all budgets. ⓐ 89 Elvet Bridge ⓣ 0191 370 9873
ⓦ www.lebeado.co.uk

🔺 *The magnificent Durham Cathedral, from the cloister*

The Mugwump Designer labels, soft toys, glassware, prints and greeting cards. ⓐ 37 Saddler Street ❶ 0191 386 1282

TAKING A BREAK

From morning coffee to gourmet eating, Durham has an excellent selection of restaurants, cafés and bars. The Walkergate complex, which houses the Gala Theatre, is a good place to start. ⓦ www.walkergate-durham.co.uk

The Undercroft Restaurant £ ❶ Located in the cloisters of Durham Cathedral, the Undercroft offers an excellent selection of home-produced food from sandwiches to traditional meals. ⓐ The Cloisters, Durham Cathedral ❶ 0191 386 3721 ⓦ www.durhamcathedral.co.uk ⓛ 10.00–16.30 daily

Gourmet Spot £££ ❷ Exciting fine dining for lovers of good food, located in idyllic surroundings just out of the centre. ⓐ The Avenue ❶ 0191 384 6655 ⓦ www.gourmet-spot.co.uk ⓛ 17.00–late Tues–Sat

● *QuayLink buses are a good way to get around Newcastle*

PRACTICAL
information

Directory

GETTING THERE & GETTING AROUND
By air
Newcastle International Airport is used by many of the major airlines, including BA and easyJet. There are regular flights from London (Stansted and Heathrow), Belfast and Bristol. The airport is 11 km (7 miles) northwest of Newcastle centre. The Tyne and Wear Metro system operates regular services from the airport and takes you straight into the city centre. Metro trains leave every 12 minutes and the journey time is 25 minutes. Buses (X77, X78 and X79) take 18 minutes to Eldon Square and run every 30 minutes Monday to Saturday. The taxi fare to central Newcastle is, at the time of writing, about £18. There are several car rental offices in the Arrivals Hall as well as a bureau de change and an information desk.

British Airways Ⓦ www.britishairways.com
easyJet Ⓦ www.easyjet.com

Many people are aware that air travel emits CO_2, which contributes to climate change. You may be interested in the possibility of lessening the environmental impact of your flight through the charity **Climate Care** (Ⓦ www.jpmorganclimatecare. com), which offsets your CO_2 by funding environmental projects around the world.

One way of helping to reduce the environmental impact of your flight is to buy carbon offsets through the Climate Care charity, which then funds environmental projects with the proceeds. Visit Ⓦ www.jpmorganclimatecare.com for further details.

By rail

If you are travelling to Newcastle from London or the southeast, then the train from King's Cross, which takes around three hours, has to be the most comfortable and pleasant way of doing this. At peak times there are trains every 15–30 minutes. From Manchester it takes less than 3 hours, with a change at York, while from Edinburgh the journey time is about 1 hour 35 minutes.

East Coast Trains ⓦ www.eastcoast.co.uk
Virgin Trains ⓦ www.virgintrains.co.uk

By car

Newcastle is approached from the north by the A1 trunk road and the south by the A1 and A1(M), and there are signs to the city centre from both directions. From the south take the A184 exit (Gateshead and Newcastle Centre) crossing over the Redheugh Bridge into Newcastle, and from the north take the City Centre and Airport exit at Gosforth Park, and follow the A167 into Newcastle through Gosforth.

HEALTH, SAFETY & CRIME

The only Accident and Emergency Department in the city is based at the General Hospital on Westgate Road, well out of the city centre. There is a walk-in centre next door to the A & E Department, with an out-of-hours GP service, but minor injuries can be treated from 09.00–16.00 daily at the Royal Victoria Infirmary (RVI) on Queen Victoria Road, just west of the Haymarket. There is also an Eye Casualty Department at the RVI, open from 08.30–16.30 Monday to Friday and

09.00–11.30 on Saturday. Another walk-in centre can be found in the Jurys Inn complex. Further details can be found at Ⓦ www.newcastle-hospitals.org.uk and Ⓦ www.newcastlecentralwalkincentre.co.uk/site.

Crime is no more a problem in Newcastle than in any other UK city and, because most of the places you will be likely to visit are in well-frequented areas, it is arguably safer than most.

TOILETS

There are public toilets in Newcastle in Eldon Square, Monument Mall and the Grainger Market. All the museums and galleries have good toilet facilities, as do the City Library (see page 69), cafés and bars, as well as department stores.

CHILDREN

Newcastle is generally a child-friendly city, and there are enough child-friendly cafés and restaurants throughout the city to keep even the hungriest of youngsters satisfied. All the museums and the art galleries have exhibits aimed specifically at younger age groups, although they are not specifically catered for in The Sage or BALTIC Centres. Tours are available around St James' Park (see pages 67–8) which will be a thrill for aspiring footballers, and probably for some of their dads too! Finally, the City Pool (see page 21) is always a great source of fun for the whole family.

TRAVELLERS WITH DISABILITIES

Travellers with disabilities are well catered for in Newcastle. Both Eldon Square and Eldon Garden shopping centres offer a Shopmobility scheme with special parking arrangements in the

Eldon Garden multi-storey car park. Adjacent car parks have designated places for orange/blue badge-holders. For further information, go to ⓦ www.eldon-square.co.uk/shopmobility.htm. Museums and galleries have also gone to great lengths to ensure accessibility. For further information, go to ⓦ www.twmuseums.org.uk/about/accessibility. Historical buildings present a problem, however, and the Castle Keep, for example, can only accept visitors with disabilities to the Garrison Room on the ground floor, and that by appointment only.

FURTHER INFORMATION

There are two Tourist Information Centres in Newcastle, one in Grainger Town and the other on the Quayside. In both centres you can obtain a map of the city and other useful information free of charge. They also sell tickets for city walking tours, open-top bus trips and river cruises. ⓦ www.riverescapes.co.uk

Central Arcade Tourist Information Centre

ⓐ 8–9 Central Arcade ⓣ 0191 277 8000 ⓛ 09.30–17.30 Mon–Fri, 09.00–17.30 Sat, closed Sun

The Guildhall Tourist Information Centre

ⓐ Quayside ⓣ 0191 277 8000 ⓛ 10.00–17.00 Mon–Fri, 09.00–17.00 Sat, 09.00–16.00 Sun ⓔ tourist.info@newcastle.gov.uk

Useful websites include:
ⓦ www.newcastle.gov.uk and follow the link to Leisure Libraries and Tourism ⓦ www.visitnewcastlegateshead.com the official website of NewcastleGateshead.

ACKNOWLEDGEMENTS
The photographs in this book were taken by Cezare White for Thomas Cook Publishing, to whom the copyright belongs, except for the following: iStockphoto pages 10, 56 (Alan Crawford), 81 (Arno Jansen).

Project editor: Tom Lee
Copy editor: Penny Isaac
Proofreaders: Rosemary Moore & Emma Haigh
Layout: Julie Crane
Indexer: Penelope Kent

AUTHOR BIOGRAPHY
Newcastle born and bred Paul Shawcross has been a travel journalist for over twenty years, writing guidebooks and magazine articles that normally feature the sunnier climes of southern Europe. However he does occasionally pen pieces about his native northeast and, as a proud Geordie, writing about his home town is always a great pleasure.

Send your thoughts to
books@thomascook.com

- Found a great bar, club, shop or must-see sight that we don't feature?
- Like to tip us off about any information that needs a little updating?
- Want to tell us what you love about this handy little guidebook and more importantly how we can make it even handier?

Then here's your chance to tell all! Send us ideas, discoveries and recommendations today and then look out for your valuable input in the next edition of this title.

Email the above address (stating the title) or write to:
pocket guides Series Editor, Thomas Cook Publishing, PO Box 227, Coningsby Road, Peterborough PE3 8SB, UK.